BE ING AS LEAD ING

YOUR ROADMAP TO SHAPING CULTURE THROUGH LIFE'S DISRUPTIONS

DR.KENDRA MOMON

STUDY GUIDE

BE ING AS LEAD ING

YOUR ROADMAP TO SHAPING CULTURE THROUGH LIFE'S DISRUPTIONS

DR. KENDRA MOMON

STUDY GUIDE

AVAIL

CONTENTS

chapter 1

REWIND

"We get so consumed by our fast-paced, quick-fix, hurry-up-and-wait, 100mph consumer culture that our to-do lists lead us."

READING TIME

Read Chapter 1: "Rewind," in *Being As Leading,* reflect on the questions and discuss your answers with your study group.

In general, how do you define "culture"?

_____

_____

_____

_____

_____

_____

_____

How does the definition change as your location and/or environment changes?

_____

_____

_____

_____

_____

_____

How has your idea of "culture" changed over time?

_____

_____

_____

_____

_____

_____

_____

REFLECT ON

Luke 10:38-42 (NLT):

As Jesus and the disciples continued on their way to Jerusalem, they came to a certain village where a woman named Martha welcomed him into her home. Her sister, Mary, sat at the Lord's feet, listening to what he taught. But Martha was distracted by the big dinner she was preparing. She came to Jesus and said, "Lord, doesn't it seem unfair to you that my sister just sits here while I do all the work? Tell her to come and help me." But the Lord said to her, "My dear Martha, you are worried and upset over all these details! There is only one thing worth being concerned about. Mary has discovered it, and it will not be taken away from her."

Describe a culture clash that has occurred in your life. What happened before, during, and after?

_____

_____

_____

_____

In what ways has your culture influenced your being and vice-versa?

_____

_____

_____

_____

How does mankind having been made in the Imago Dei impact your culture close to home and in the office? What about within your community and throughout your state/country?

_____

_____

_____

_____

If you are a Christ follower, how has that culture influenced your being? How might it be beneficial for your being to influence that culture?

_____

_____

_____

_____

_____

How can you tell if you are more likely to "do" or to "be"?

_____

_____

_____

_____

_____

_____

How good are you at being still and knowing that God is working your circumstances for His glory?

_____

_____

_____

_____

_____

_____

How does culture influence your ability to be still and know?

_____

_____

_____

_____

_____

chapter 2

CULTURE AND LEADERSHIP

"As shared, culture is a difficult term to define as it means different things and connotes different nuances to different people."

READING TIME

Read Chapter 2: "Culture and Leadership," in *Being As Leading,* reflect on the questions and discuss your answers with your study group.

Based on the definition of culture as "the way of life, customs, and script of a group of people," define the following cultures: your institution; you as an individual; you as a person interdependent with other people.

_____

_____

_____

_____

_____

_____

How does your culture influence what you wear, eat, speak, and believe?

_____

_____

_____

_____

_____

_____

REFLECT ON

Matthew 20:20-28:

Then the mother of Zebedee's sons came to Jesus with her sons and, kneeling down, asked a favor of him. "What is it you want?" he asked. She said, "Grant that one of these two sons of mine may sit at your right and the other at your left in your kingdom." "You don't know what you are asking," Jesus said to them. "Can you drink the cup I am going to drink?" "We can," they answered. Jesus said to them, "You will indeed drink from my cup, but to sit at my right or left is not for me to grant. These places belong to those for whom they have been prepared by my Father." When the ten heard about this, they were indignant with the two brothers. Jesus called them together and said, "You know that the rulers of the Gentiles lord it over them, and their high officials exercise authority over them. Not so with you. Instead, whoever wants to become great among you must be your servant, and whoever wants to be first must be your slave—just as the Son of Man did not come to be served, but to serve, and to give his life as a ransom for many."

How does your public culture manifest differently than your private culture?

_____

_____

_____

_____

_____

_____

Do you agree with this statement? "Combined, leadership and culture organize the thoughts, feelings, values, and outcomes of people, leaders, institutions, communities, and organizations." Why or why not?

_____

_____

_____

_____

_____

_____

How does the previous statement apply to you as a leader in your institution, community, or organization?

_____

_____

_____

_____

_____

_____

How do you intentionally guide others toward your particular end?

_____

_____

_____

_____

_____

With which traditional model of leadership are you most familiar: Great Man, Trait, or Management Theory? What do you see as the pros and cons of each?

_____

_____

_____

_____

_____

_____

_____

_____

What experience do you have with Participative, Transformative, and Authentic Leadership? What do you see as the pros and cons of each?

_____

_____

_____

_____

How does your institution, community, or organization lend itself to Servant-Leadership?

_____

_____

_____

_____

_____

_____

FOR THE CULTURE

"As quiet as it is kept, overlooked, and even ignored, there is the obvious and inevitable reality of culture. It changes. Absolutely, unequivocally, and even predictably, culture will and must change."

READING TIME

Read Chapter 3: "For the Culture," in *Being As Leading*, reflect on the questions and discuss your answers with your study group.

Which cultures can you think of that have changed dramatically over the years? How have they changed?

_____

_____

_____

_____

_____

_____

How susceptible are you and/or your organization to "trends" in culture? How have those trends worked for and against you?

_____

_____

_____

_____

_____

_____

REFLECT ON

Acts 17:16-21 (NIV) and how it relates to current cultural movements:

While Paul was waiting for them in Athens, he was greatly distressed to see that the city was full of idols. So he reasoned in the synagogue with both Jews and God-fearing Greeks, as well as in the marketplace day by day with those who happened to be there. A group of Epicurean and Stoic philosophers began to debate with him. Some of them asked, "What is this babbler trying to say?" Others remarked, "He seems to be advocating foreign gods." They said this because Paul was preaching the good news about Jesus and the resurrection. Then they took him and brought him to a meeting of the Areopagus, where they said to him, "May we know what this new teaching is that you are presenting? You are bringing some strange ideas to our ears, and we would like to know what they mean." (All the Athenians and the foreigners who lived there spent their time doing nothing but talking about and listening to the latest ideas.)

How influential is social media to your organization? Have you benefited from likes, retweets, or clicks? If so, how?

_____

_____

_____

_____

_____

What hashtag movements are you familiar with? What have those movements tried to bring to the forefront of human consciousness?

_____

_____

_____

_____

_____

In your opinion, what are some current "hot-button" topics or issues that have been prevalent on social media?

_____

_____

_____

_____

_____

As a leader, how could you direct your church, organization, or institution to respond to "hot-button" topics in such a way that your presentation doesn't get visceral?

_____

_____

_____

_____

"Culture is supposed to be an articulator. However, devoid of change, often it becomes an artifact."

What activities has your organization engaged in "for the culture"? Did these activities work the way you thought they would?

_____

_____

_____

_____

_____

_____

What are some pros and cons of the #canceled culture movement? How does canceling people and organizations affect the business bottom line?

_____

_____

_____

_____

_____

_____

Do you agree with Dr. Martin L. King Jr's., statement from "A Time to Break Silence"? "And some of us who have already begun to break the silence of the night have found that the calling to speak is often a vocation of agony, but we must speak. We must speak with all the humility that is appropriate to our limited vision, but we must speak." Why or why not?

_____

_____

_____

_____

_____

_____

YOU ARE A CULTURE OF ONE

"The truth of the matter is that culture—as powerful and pervasive as it is—shouldn't dominate us as much as it should be influenced, informed, created, and shaped by us."

Read Chapter 4: "You Are A Culture of One," in *Being As Leading,* reflect on the questions and discuss your answers with your study group.

Do you agree with the following statement? "Given the magnitude of its scope and reach, I think it's fair to say that culture isn't just a way of life, culture is life!" Why or why not?

_____

_____

_____

_____

_____

_____

Has your culture—in any arena—dictated and/or influenced your values, beliefs, and behaviors?

_____

_____

_____

_____

_____

REFLECT ON

Philippians 4:4-9 (NIV). Compare it to your culture-of-one thought patterns.

Rejoice in the Lord always. I will say it again: Rejoice! Let your gentleness be evident to all. The Lord is near. Do not be anxious about anything, but in every situation, by prayer and petition, with thanksgiving, present your requests to God. And the peace of God, which transcends all understanding, will guard your hearts and your minds in Christ Jesus.

Finally, brothers and sisters, whatever is true, whatever is noble, whatever is right, whatever is pure, whatever is lovely, whatever is admirable—if anything is excellent or praiseworthy—think about such things. Whatever you have learned or received or heard from me, or seen in me—put it into practice. And the God of peace will be with you.

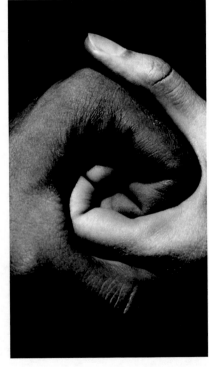

In which ways have you resisted culture's influence on you and/or your organization?

_____

_____

_____

_____

_____

_____

_____

_____

To what extent is your culture of one authentic and congruent?

_____

_____

_____

_____

_____

_____

_____

_____

In what ways have you had to set the tone, pace, and environment of your institution's culture?

_____

_____

_____

_____

_____

_____

_____

"Lastly, you are a culture of one in the legacy you create. What do you do now while you are still alive and present on the earth to impact people?"

How well-defined are your intentions, motives, and ways of being and thinking? What have you done or could you do to ensure everyone around you knows them?

_____

_____

_____

_____

_____

_____

_____

_____

_____

_____

Which of the 10 cultural clues in this chapter are most challenging for you? Which are easiest for you?

_____

_____

_____

_____

_____

_____

_____

_____

_____

_____

How well does your organization's culture reflect your personal culture? What could be improved to make the two more congruent?

_____

_____

_____

_____

_____

_____

How does your heart impact your leadership style? How comfortable would you be if others followed you the way you follow Jesus?

_____

_____

_____

_____

_____

_____

chapter 5

BE A CULTURAL ANTHROPOLOGIST

*"It is in our being that we have freedom to lead
from the seat of authority and unique wiring that
God has handcrafted specifically in you and me."*

READING TIME

Read Chapter 5: "Be A Cultural Anthropologist," in *Being As Leading,* reflect on the questions and discuss your answers with your study group.

In what ways has God handcrafted you specifically for the role you play in your organization?

_____

_____

_____

_____

_____

_____

What would applying the field of anthropology look like in your organization? Think in terms of archaeology, linguistics, physical anthropology, and cultural anthropology.

_____

_____

_____

_____

_____

_____

REFLECT ON

John 10:1-6 (NIV):

"Very truly I tell you Pharisees, anyone who does not enter the sheep pen by the gate, but climbs in by some other way, is a thief and a robber. The one who enters by the gate is the shepherd of the sheep. The gatekeeper opens the gate for him, and the sheep listen to his voice. He calls his own sheep by name and leads them out. When he has brought out all his own, he goes on ahead of them, and his sheep follow him because they know his voice. But they will never follow a stranger; in fact, they will run away from him because they do not recognize a stranger's voice." Jesus used this figure of speech, but the Pharisees did not understand what he was telling them.

Which of the following seven data compilation methods could you implement in your organization, and how? Participant observation; in-depth interviews; focus groups; textual analysis; field work; modeling; comparative study.

_____

_____

_____

_____

_____

_____

Do you agree with the following statement? "I believe that in order to be effective cultural anthropologists, we have to study the language, traditions, customs, and behaviors within our organizations, groups, and circles." Why or why not?

_____

_____

_____

_____

_____

_____

What have you done intuitively to study the people you lead? What did this process of study look like?

_____

_____

_____

_____

_____

_____

If your organization has not studied itself, what has prevented it? Time? Cost? Mess? Fear? What would be the worst-case scenario of performing a dig?

_____

_____

_____

_____

_____

_____

If Margaret Mead is correct, and "What people say, what people do, and what they say they do are entirely different things," what is your organization's protocol for inspecting what it expects?

_____

_____

_____

_____

_____

What benefits could you reap if you "participate, observe, and learn" during an organizational dig?

_____

_____

_____

_____

_____

_____

In what ways does your church, institution, or organization value people and morale over titles, positions, and practices? How could it do better?

_____

_____

_____

_____

_____

chapter 6

FOLLOW ME

*"When we, like Kanye West, invite others to engage
in "Follow Me" being as leading culture, we are
providing an open door to where we currently find
ourselves in authenticity, transparency, and clarity."*

Read Chapter 6: "Follow Me," in *Being As Leading,* reflect on the questions and discuss your answers with your study group.

What is your gut reaction when you think about leading your followers from a place of authenticity, transparency, and clarity?

_____

_____

_____

_____

_____

_____

In general, how does your institution, organization, or church navigate change?

_____

_____

_____

_____

_____

REFLECT ON

The exchange between Jesus and the disciples in Matthew 4:18-20 (AMP):

As Jesus was walking by the Sea of Galilee, He noticed two brothers, Simon who was called Peter, and Andrew his brother, casting a net into the sea; for they were fishermen. And He said to them, "Follow Me [as My disciples, accepting Me as your Master and Teacher and walking the same path of life that I walk], and I will make you fishers of men." Immediately they left their nets and followed Him [becoming His disciples, believing and trusting in Him and following His example].

When has your organization been subject to paralysis or regression? What caused it? How did your organization overcome this state?

_____

_____

_____

_____

_____

_____

What "exchange" does your organization offer its members that makes them willing to function beyond the status quo?

_____

_____

_____

_____

_____

_____

Do you agree with the following statement? "In issuing any call today, leaders have to be clear about their objectives and outcome so that others are aware of what is at stake if they are to follow the leader." Why or why not?

_____

_____

_____

_____

_____

_____

SHARE YOUR STORY

"As cultural anthropologists, we must be painstakingly careful to recognize, correct, and close any ideological or ethical gaps in the idealized self/organizational cultural in comparison to the actual self/organizational culture we perpetuate."

What are the predominant characteristics of your leadership/organizational culture? How does your organization make them clear?

_____

_____

_____

_____

What can you do to make sure the systems are in place, so you can effectively reinforce expectations and outcomes?

_____

_____

_____

_____

Is your organization people- or profit-driven? How can you tell?

_____

_____

_____

_____

Does your personal bent lean toward oblique or obvious thinking? Which is more productive for your organization? What can you do to grow more of a Follow Me culture?

_____

_____

_____

_____

chapter 7

LOVE AND COVER OTHERS

"If we are going to serve others as faithful stewards, we must each first attend to and be the faithful steward of our own soul."

READING TIME

Read Chapter 7: "Love and Cover Others," in *Being As Leading,* reflect on the questions and discuss your answers with your study group.

Is your natural bent to follow the letter of the law or the spirit of the law? How does that manifest?

_____

_____

_____

_____

_____

_____

What causes you to fly on autopilot? What does your autopilot look like? How do people respond to it?

_____

_____

_____

_____

_____

_____

REFLECT ON

1 Peter 4:7-12 (NIV):

The end of all things is near. Therefore be alert and of sober mind so that you may pray. Above all, love each other deeply, because love covers over a multitude of sins. Offer hospitality to one another without grumbling. Each of you should use whatever gift you have received to serve others, as faithful stewards of God's grace in its various forms. If anyone speaks, they should do so as one who speaks the very words of God. If anyone serves, they should do so with the strength God provides, so that in all things God may be praised through Jesus Christ. To him be the glory and the power for ever and ever. Amen.

Do you agree with this statement? "One of the things I was reminded of is that until we face what has hindered our ability to be, we can't effectively love and lead others." Why or why not?

_____

_____

_____

_____

_____

_____

_____

How do you know when your heart and your head are out of alignment? What have you been able to do to realign them?

_____

_____

_____

_____

_____

_____

_____

Are there areas in your life where your ability to lead from the core and essence of your being is limited, hindered, blocked, or knowingly compartmentalized? What are they?

_____

_____

_____

_____

_____

_____

_____

How would you encourage someone who is desperately trying to lead from his or her place of being but experiences periods of inhospitality or failure?

_____
_____
_____
_____
_____

How are you doing with covering others? Who do you cover? How do you cover those people? What do their needs and your coverings for them look like?

_____
_____
_____
_____
_____

When have you failed to lead from a place of genuineness? How did it affect your ability to see people through the Imago Dei?

_____
_____
_____
_____
_____

Since choosing to lead from a place of being takes vulnerability and courage, how do you plan to strengthen your being so you can lead for the long term?

_____

_____

_____

_____

_____

THE 3 M'S: MINDSETS, MICROAGGRESSIONS, AND MISUNDERSTANDINGS

"Change is unavoidable.... Conflict is also an inescapable part of our leadership, workplace, and family life. It's a part of culture."

Read
Chapter 8:
"The 3 M's:
Mindsets,
Microag-
gressions,
and Misun-
derstand-
ings," in
*Being As
Leading,*
reflect on
the ques-
tions and
discuss your
answers
with your
study group.

Do you prefer change or conflict in your leadership culture? Why is one easier than the other?

_____

_____

_____

_____

_____

What subjects/issues are most likely to cause conflict in your organization, institution, or church? Where do they fall on the spectrum of the six key indicators of conflict: unconscious bias, social intelligence, preexisting mindsets, in-groups/out-groups, power dynamics, and norms and practices?

_____

_____

_____

_____

_____

REFLECT ON

Romans 12:9-18 (NIV):

Love must be sincere. Hate what is evil; cling to what is good. Be devoted to one another in love. Honor one another above yourselves. Never be lacking in zeal, but keep your spiritual fervor, serving the Lord. Be joyful in hope, patient in affliction, faithful in prayer. Share with the Lord's people who are in need. Practice hospitality.

Bless those who persecute you; bless and do not curse. Rejoice with those who rejoice; mourn with those who mourn. Live in harmony with one another. Do not be proud, but be willing to associate with people of low position. Do not be conceited.

Do not repay anyone evil for evil. Be careful to do what is right in the eyes of everyone. If it is possible, as far as it depends on you, live at peace with everyone.

How have your people traditionally dealt with their disagreements? What avenues have been built into your leadership culture so people can discuss and resolve conflict without war, violence, and death?

_____

_____

_____

_____

_____

_____

Is your mindset more fixed- or growth-oriented? What past history and experiences, as well as current realities, have shaped it?

_____

_____

_____

_____

_____

_____

What is the overall mindset of your organizational community? How can you—as a leader—ask the hard questions so you can bolster potentially negative thought processes?

_____

_____

_____

_____

_____

_____

"Conflict is certain because at its base and safest level, it's merely a difference in perspective of how two people view the same situation."

What is your personal experience with microaggressions? How have you dealt with people attempting to demean or demoralize you or those you lead?

_____

_____

_____

_____

_____

How can you make your organizational environment more sensitive to microaggressions, so all of your members feel their voices are heard and your leadership strength authentically empowers the less powerful?

_____

_____

_____

_____

_____

What are your organization's biggest challenges in the area of communication? What procedures do you have in place to prevent and clear-up miscommunications?

_____

_____

_____

_____

_____

chapter 9

EQ, GQ, AND YOU!

"If we are going to create healthy, transformative, and pay-it-forward leadership cultures, we must provide a blueprint for how to overcome leadership-culture corruptors and replace them with leadership-culture creators and multipliers."

How emotionally intelligent do you think you are? Rate yourself on a scale of 1-10 (with 1 being "I never exhibit this attribute" and 10 being "I always exhibit this attribute").

_____ Self-awareness

_____ Self-management

_____ Social-awareness

_____ Social Skills

What can you do to make your lowest-rated emotional-intelligence attribute higher? How might this help you in your leadership role? How will it help those who follow you?

_____

_____

_____

_____

_____

_____

REFLECT ON

Philippians 4:1 and 8. How does it speak to you about the importance of your "quotients" as they pertain to your leadership position?

My dear, dear friends! I love you so much. I do want the very best for you. You make me feel such joy, fill me with such pride. Don't waver. Stay on track, steady in God. ...Summing it all up, friends, I'd say you'll do best by filling your minds and meditating on things true, noble, reputable, authentic, compelling, gracious—the best, not the worst; the beautiful, not the ugly; things to praise, not things to curse. Put into practice what you learned from me, what you heard and saw and realized. Do that, and God, who makes everything work together, will work you into his most excellent harmonies.

What type of motives are ego-driven?

_____

_____

_____

_____

_____

_____

Do you agree with the following statement? "While one's intelligence quotient remains the most traditional standard of aptitude, the measurement of one's cognitive ability in comparison to one's age doesn't always equate to the development and emergence of leaders who are healthy, whole, and fit to lead well." Why or why not?

_____

_____

_____

_____

_____

_____

What prevents your GQ—God Quotient—from being full-strength? How can you strengthen it, so you truly do "walk it like you talk it"?

_____

_____

_____

_____

_____

_____

In what context have you been admonished to "Be the Change"? What did the person mean who said it? Did you embrace it?

_____

_____

_____

_____

_____

What did Dr. Martin Luther King, Jr., mean when he said, "If I cannot do great things, I can do small things in a great way"?

_____

_____

_____

_____

_____

Where do you find your loudest detractors? Do those detractors fit the description of those who profit from chaos, confusion, and economic, political, racial, social, and cultural divides?

_____

_____

_____

_____

_____

How can leading from a place of being help you tune them out?

_____

_____

_____

_____

_____

_____

What has been your experience with the millennials in your institution, organization, or church? How has their presence lent itself to an intergenerational, interconnected, and intersectional body?

_____

_____

_____

_____

_____